FRANCES WELSH

TUTANKHAMUN'S EGYPT

Second edition

SHIRE EGYPTOLOGY

Cover illustration
Gold funerary mask of Tutankhamun.
(Photograph: Frances Welsh. Egyptian Antiquities Museum, Cairo.)

British Library Cataloguing in Publication Data:
Welsh, Frances
Tutankhamun's Egypt.
– (Shire Egyptology; no. 19)
1. Tutankhamen, King of Egypt
2. Egypt – Civilization – To 332 B.C.
I. Title. 932'.014
ISBN-13: 978 0 7478 0665 3.

Published in 2007 by
SHIRE PUBLICATIONS LTD
Cromwell House, Church Street, Princes Risborough,
Buckinghamshire HP27 9AA, UK.

Series Editor: Angela P. Thomas.

Number 19 in the Shire Egyptology series.

ISBN 978 0 7478 0665 3.

First published 1993. Second edition, revised and
illustrated in colour, 2007.

Printed in Malta by
Gutenberg Press Limited, Gudja Road, Tarxien PLA 19, Malta.

Contents

Acknowledgements

I wish to express my thanks to the late Mrs Barbara Adams for her support; also to colleagues and friends whose encouragement has enabled me to complete this project. I am grateful to both Mrs Amélie Kuhrt and Professor H. S. Smith, who encouraged and helped me while I was studying at University College London.

My husband, Reg, has given me unfailing support throughout and I wish to thank him for help with the illustrations and comments on the text. We are both grateful to the hospitable people of Egypt for help in visiting sites and studying their history. I also thank Peter Clayton, who has kindly provided many photographs, and the Griffith Institute for permission to reproduce photographs taken by Harry Burton during excavation. Acknowledgement is also made to W. J. Murnane and Penguin Books for the chronology.

List of illustrations

Chronology

Based on W. J. Murnane, *The Penguin Guide to Ancient Egypt,* 1983, and including names of rulers mentioned in the text.

Predynastic	before 3150 BC		
Early Dynastic	3150-2686 BC		Dynasties I to II
Old Kingdom	2686-2181 BC		Dynasties III to VI
First Intermediate Period	2181-2040 BC		Dynasties VII to XI
Middle Kingdom	2040-1782 BC		Dynasties XI to XII
Second Intermediate Period	1782-1570 BC		Dynasties XIII to XVII
New Kingdom	1570-1070 BC		
		1570-1293	Dynasty XVIII
		1570-1546	*Ahmose*
		1551-1524	*Amenhotep I*
		1524-1518	*Tuthmosis I*
		1518-1504	*Tuthmosis II*
		1504-1450	*Tuthmosis III*
		1498-1483	*Hatshepsut (?)*
		1453-1419	*Amenhotep II*
		1419-1386	*Tuthmosis IV*
		1386-1349	*Amenhotep III*
		1350-1334	*Amenhotep IV / Akhenaten*
		1336-1334	*Smenkhkare*
		1334-1325	*Tutankhamun*
		1325-1321	*Ay*
		1321-1293	*Horemheb*
		1293-1185	Dynasty XIX
		1293-1291	*Ramesses I*
		1291-1278	*Seti I*
		1279-1212	*Ramesses II*
		1185-1070	Dynasty XX
		1182-1151	*Ramesses III*
Third Intermediate Period	1070-713 BC		Dynasties XXI to XXIV
Late Period	713-332 BC		Dynasties XXV to XXXI
Graeco-Roman Period	332BC-AD 395		Ptolemies and Roman Emperors

1

Introduction

On 4th November 1922 the top step of a stone stairway was uncovered in a remote desert valley in Upper Egypt. Sixteen steps led down to a tomb with an intact burial chamber containing the mummified body of an obscure Pharaoh named Tutankhamun, together with funerary equipment of such great quantity and richness as to astonish both archaeologist and layman.

This was not a chance find by treasure seekers: it was the result of searches sustained over many years by a series of archaeologists and scholars, the final one being the meticulous excavator, Howard Carter.

However, finding his tomb did not mean that Tutankhamun was 'discovered': many aspects of his life and reign still remained unknown and some of the material in his tomb posed new problems. Egyptologists have looked for solutions from other excavations and from fresh interpretation of known material but many decades later the personality of Tutankhamun and the events of his life remain uncertain. Because the contents of the tomb were carefully recorded the material culture of the time in which he lived is well known but the historical events of the reign are conjectural and open to reinterpretation.

Before 1922 knowledge of Tutankhamun derived from a few objects in museums and at sites in Egypt (figure 1). W. Flinders Petrie wrote: 'Of this reign we know scarcely anything, except from the fine tomb of Hui' (Theban tomb no. 40 Huya), in which painted scenes indicated that Nubia was under firm control. Several small objects, such as rings, pendants, knob handles, kohl tubes and a wooden cubit rod, bore his throne name 'Nebkheperure', as did some blocks at the temples of Amun and Mut at Karnak. The burial of an Apis bull at Saqqara in his reign was recorded on a stela in the Serapeum. It was known that Tutankhamun's queen was Ankhsenamun, the third daughter of Akhenaten and Nefertiti, and that both their names had originally included the name of the god Aten. But his position in history was unclear because the cartouche of Tutankhamun did not appear in the Ramesside King Lists, in which Horemheb was treated as the direct successor of Amenhotep III.

A stela found in 1905 at Karnak described how the Aten cult was abandoned, the worship of Amun revived and traditional political organisation restored. Close study revealed that this stela (usually called the Restoration Stela) had been set up originally by Nebkheperure Tutankhamun, whose names had been replaced by those of Horemheb. The inscription carved on a granite lion statue from Soleb referring to his 'father (or ancestor) Nebmaatre Amenhotep' (Amenhotep III) stated his claim of descent from a king who ruled before the heresy of Akhenaten.

By 1922, then, although Tutankhamun's parents had not been identified, his name and that of his wife were known, as well as those of her parents. His position in history was established. He was known to have initiated the return to orthodoxy after the death of Akhenaten but the length of his reign, its events and significance were obscure. His age and personality were completely unknown. The eminent Egyptologist Arthur Weigall speculated as late as November 1923 that he could have been Akhenaten's ageing court chamberlain, Tutu, or perhaps a dwarf because a small chair had been found in the Antechamber of his tomb.

The search

Excavations in the Valley of the Kings at Thebes in the early twentieth century uncovered tombs, coffins, mummies and funerary equipment which yielded information about the Pharaohs of the New Kingdom. Although there was no reference in ancient texts to Tutankhamun's burial and no tomb or mummy had been found for him, Howard Carter believed that the king had been buried at Thebes following his return to traditional religious practices.

There were three pieces of evidence which suggested that his tomb was located in the central part of the Valley (figure 2).

In 1905 Theodore Davis and Edward Ayrton had found two caches: one, beneath a rock near the tomb of Horemheb, contained a small cup of light blue faience bearing the cartouche of Nebkheperure, and in the other, in a nearby pit, were found fragments of gold foil showing Tutankhamun hunting in his chariot and slaughtering a bound enemy in front of Ankhsenamun.

In 1907 Davis and Ayrton excavated tomb KV55, which contained burial equipment of members of the Amarna royal family. This had accompanied at least two mummies which seem to have been reburied by Tutankhamun, whose name appeared on clay sealings. The identity, age and sex of the only body remaining in the tomb was not certain.

A third cache of material which included references to Tutankhamun was found by Davis in 1908 but it was only some years later that Herbert Winlock, who had realised its significance, was able to examine it. In about twelve pottery storage jars were found broken

1. Colossal pink sandstone statue of Amun wearing the plumed crown, with features of Tutankhamun; at Karnak Temple. (Photograph by Frances Welsh.)

2. Tomb of Tutankhamun (foreground) in the Valley of the Kings, Thebes, with the entrance to the tomb of Ramesses V and VI behind. (Photograph by Frances Welsh.)

pottery drinking cups and wine jars; broad collars of flowers and leaves sewn on a papyrus base; two small hand brooms; the bones of animals and birds; a brightly painted miniature funerary mask; bags of natron salts and chaff; and bandages, some of them tightly rolled, which had been torn from used domestic linen. A torn linen sheet was marked 'Year 8 of the Lord of the Two Lands Nebkheperure' and sealings showed his name associated with the priests of the royal necropolis. All this appeared to be embalmers' debris together with the remains of a funerary feast consumed by eight people as a final ritual act of farewell to the deceased Tutankhamun, and this led Carter to seek the Pharaoh's burial in the area between the tombs of Seti I and Ramesses VI.

Carter's patron, Lord Carnarvon, began working in the Valley in 1917. Although previous excavators had declared that nothing remained to be found there, Carter noticed that a small section near the tomb of Ramesses VI had never been investigated. Methodical clearance down to bedrock revealed a series of workmen's huts standing on a mass of flint boulders and, beneath these, a tomb entrance.

The tomb discovered

There was no doubt that it was the tomb of Tutankhamun. The doorway at the foot of the steps was stamped with seals bearing the name of Nebkheperure within a cartouche, and when the tomb was entered there was abundant evidence that it contained the mummified body and burial equipment of Tutankhamun (figure 3).

The narrow short stairway led down to a corridor and into a rectangular room, which Carter called the Antechamber. This was filled with objects of all kinds, some from daily life and others of a funerary nature, many previously unknown, piled up in disorder and crammed together. The impression was of a storeroom rather than a royal burial. Three large gilded couches were heaped with caskets, chairs, beds, walking sticks and bows, the space below being filled with oviform boxes and more caskets, stools and a golden throne. The floor space was littered with alabaster vases, floral bouquets, caskets and a heap of dismantled chariots spilling forward from the south-east corner (figure 4). A small side room called the Annexe was crammed with similar objects.

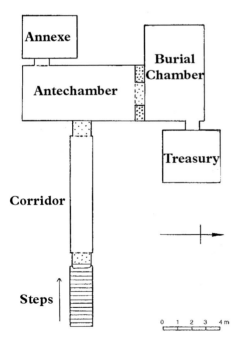

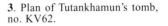

3. Plan of Tutankhamun's tomb, no. KV62.

At the north end of the Antechamber (figure 5), two life-size wooden statues of the king guarded the sealed entrance to the Burial Chamber, which contained the first intact royal burial to be seen by modern Egyptologists.

The room was completely filled by four gilded funerary shrines, nesting one within the other, protecting the stone sarcophagus, which contained three coffins, the two outer ones gilded, the innermost of gold. In this lay the mummified body of Nebkheperure Tutankhamun overlaid with jewellery and amulets and a magnificent portrait mask of gold. Objects and symbols placed within the burial furnishings gave religious and magical protection to the dead king.

Beyond the Burial Chamber lay another small room, called by Carter the Treasury, guarded by a wooden model of the recumbent jackal god of embalming, Anubis (figure 6). This room contained a gilded shrine enclosing the canopic chest for the king's viscera

4. The southern end of the Antechamber with dismantled chariots and furniture. (Courtesy of the Griffith Institute, Oxford.)

5. The north end of the Antechamber with two draped wooden figures guarding the sealed entrance to the Burial Chamber, the funerary couch with lion heads, painted casket, bow box, floral bouquet and a bed. (From Carter and Mace, *The Tomb of Tutankhamun*, volume I, 1923, plate XVI. Courtesy of the Griffith Institute, Oxford.)

with numerous small shrines, dismantled chariots and funerary equipment. Except in the Burial Chamber, the tomb walls were undecorated. The numerous caskets and boxes in the tomb held richly decorated robes and sandals, necklaces and gold rings, sceptres and faience cups, as well as the king's underclothes and childhood toys. These were not packed carefully into appropriate boxes but appeared to have been stuffed in at random. A group of gold rings wrapped in a linen shawl lay on the floor. These and the two small caches of items bearing Tutankhamun's name found in the Valley previously, together with the small entry holes to the Annexe and the Burial Chamber, indicated that the early stage of a tomb robbery had been in progress. It was Carter's view that robbers had entered the tomb twice shortly after the interment and had taken easily portable gold items and valuable liquids such as oils and perfumes. The necropolis authorities had then hastily tidied the tomb, re-sealed the door and removed the embalmers' debris from the corridor, which was then blocked with rubble. The filled stairway and concealed entrance remained hidden when workmen's huts were erected.

The care taken by Carter and his team to excavate, record and conserve what was found made it possible for the material to be studied subsequently by specialist scholars. Excavations to discover more about Tutankhamun's reign continue, at sites as widespread as Saqqara, Amarna, Karnak and Luxor and in Nubia. Modern methods of analysis may yet provide the answer to the crucial question of the king's relationship to other members of the Eighteenth Dynasty royal family.

6. The jackal god, Anubis, draped with a child's shirt, shawl and scarf, protecting the entrance to the Treasury with canopic shrine, divine figures in shrines, boats and caskets. (Courtesy of the Griffith Institute, Oxford.)

2
The reign of Tutankhamun

Historical setting

The end of the Eighteenth Dynasty was a period of political and religious changes. Under Amenhotep III Egypt had enjoyed the wealth and prestige of empire (figure 7); the supreme state god was Amun-Re, whose cult centre at Thebes was the religious capital, while political administration was based at Memphis.

Amenhotep IV, his son, made radical changes in religious and political concepts. He moved the royal capital to Amarna in Middle Egypt, where he built the new city of Akhetaten, which he dedicated to worship of the Aten sundisk, in whose honour he changed his name to Akhenaten (figure 8). This form of sun worship overruled all other expressions of religion. Other gods were systematically eliminated and their temple endowments used to support the Aten cult, and new styles of art and architecture were introduced.

Tutankhamun's family history and upbringing and the events of his reign are difficult to establish because his close association with Akhenaten led to the destruction of records made in his lifetime and the deliberate omission of his name from later King Lists.

Although it is known that his name at birth was Tutankh*aten*, it is not certain who his parents were, nor are the place and date of his birth known. He may, perhaps, have been born at Thebes as the son of Amenhotep III and Queen Tiye, or at Amarna as the son of Akhenaten and a secondary wife, who may have been Kiya.

That Amenhotep III was his father was inferred from the inscription on the lion statue at Soleb (see above) and also from the assumption that Amenhotep III is represented by the small uninscribed gold statuette (figure 9) found in the tomb. This was placed in a nest of miniature coffins bearing Tutankhamun's name, which included a separate tiny coffinette inscribed with the name of Queen Tiye and containing a lock of her hair. This theory assumes that Amenhotep III and Akhenaten reigned jointly for twelve years and that Queen Tiye was able to bear a child in her late forties. If there was no co-regency, then it is probable that Akhenaten was Tutankhamun's father. As the Amarna royal family is shown as Akhenaten and his queen Nefertiti with a maximum of six daughters, but never with a son, it seems unlikely that Nefertiti was Tutankhamun's mother. Fragmentary inscriptions from Hermopolis imply the existence of 'a royal son of his body' of Akhenaten, who could have been

7. Amenhotep III offers to Amun, in the temple at Luxor, Hypostyle Hall. Orthodox style, in raised relief in sandstone. (Photograph by Frances Welsh.)

Tutankhaten and whose mother was Kiya, 'the king's beloved'. A scene in the Amarna royal tomb may represent the death of his mother following the birth of Tutankhaten. The absence of a clear statement by Tutankhamun about his parents may be because of the political need to dissociate himself from Akhenaten and stress his relationship with the orthodox Amenhotep III.

Tutankhaten's childhood was probably spent at Amarna enjoying the pleasures and privileges of being a member of Akhenaten's court. The newly built capital city of Akhetaten reflected the great wealth of the Egyptian empire. Luxury and artistic splendour pervaded the city and creative craftsmanship flourished. Society was dominated by the personal importance of the royal family as sole intermediaries between god and man. The traditional gods of Egypt had no visible place, although they were not forgotten by those who had accompanied Akhenaten to his new capital. Tutankhaten knew these high court officials and their children. He was probably on affectionate terms with Nefertiti's daughters and appears to have lived under her care in the Northern Palace. His role in the final years of Akhenaten's reign is unknown, but as a minor prince he would have been kept secure in the royal harem.

The deaths of Meketaten, second daughter of Akhenaten, and of the three younger princesses soon after his regnal Year 12 depleted the royal family. To strengthen his position, Akhenaten then appears to have associated himself as co-regent with Smenkhkare, who is known first as Ankhkheperure Neferneferuaten and later as Ankhkheperure Smenkhkare Djeserkhepru. It is not clear who this name represented. It may have been that of an elder brother of Tutankhaten or an elevated title for queen Nefertiti, who may have acted as co-regent or king for a short period. Meritaten, the eldest daughter of Akhenaten, appears as consort or royal supporter of Smenkhkare, while Akhenaten himself married his own third daughter, Ankhsenpaaten.

The events of this period are obscure but Akhenaten, Smenkhkare, Nefertiti and Meritaten all disappear from the historical record, leaving only two heirs from the Eighteenth Dynasty royal line, namely Tutankhaten and Ankhsenpaaten, who became Tutankhaten's wife

8. Nefertiti presents offerings to the Aten, whose hands confer blessings; in relief on a red quartzite stela fragment from Amarna. (Courtesy of the Petrie Museum of Egyptian Archaeology, University College London. UC 040.)

9. Squatting figure of a king, probably Tutankhamun, wearing a blue crown and necklace of glass beads, holding a crook and flail, cast in solid gold and suspended on a chain of plaited gold wire, from the miniature coffin containing some hair of Queen Tiye. (Cairo Museum; Carter 320.c. Photograph by Frances Welsh.)

10. Ankhsenamun, wearing pleated Amarna dress, fastens a necklace for Tutankhamun seated on a cushioned throne, both wearing jewellery as found in the tomb, in a relief on the golden shrine. (Cairo Museum; Carter 108. Drawing by R. B. Welsh.)

at the time of his accession (figure 10). Marriage to the surviving daughter and Great Royal Heiress of Akhenaten strengthened Tutankhaten's claim to the throne, which was based on his descent from Amenhotep III.

Political control appears to have been in the hands of high officials of the previous Amarna administration, who wished to maintain stability in Egypt. The transition from one king's reign to the next was often a volatile period, but the deaths of most members of the royal family before Akhenaten's changes had been fully established produced a dangerous situation. Both the vizier, Ay, who controlled the civil administration of Egypt, and Horemheb, who controlled the army and the northern part of the country, were prepared to support a claimant with legitimate connections to the recognised royal line.

'King of Upper and Lower Egypt' Nebkheperure

Tutankhaten's coronation probably took place at Memphis soon after his accession, but he and his court remained in residence at Amarna, where the Aten cult may have continued (figure 11).

11. Kiosk-shaped pectoral with Tutankhamun (centre), perhaps at his coronation, wearing the blue crown and jubilee robe and holding royal sceptres, standing to face Ptah (on right), who gives him life and dominion, with Sekhmet behind, who wishes him a reign of thousands of years; gold, silver, quartzite and coloured glass. (Cairo Museum; Carter 267.q. Photograph courtesy of Peter Clayton.)

12. Right armrest of the golden throne (outer face), showing *Tutankhaten* in cartouche protected by the wings of the cobra goddess Wadjet. See figures 22 and 30. (Cairo Museum; Carter 91. Photograph courtesy of Peter Clayton.)

13. Tutankhamun wearing the *atef* crown between Mut and Amun, in a triad statue from Karnak Temple. (Cairo Museum. CG.42097. Photograph by Frances Welsh.)

14. Tutankhamun offers to Amun at Luxor Temple (rear of Pylon 2), with Horemheb's names in cartouches; sandstone relief. (Photograph by Frances Welsh.)

However, in its extreme form the cult was the personal obsession of an established adult Pharaoh able to override opposition: it had little to offer non-royal individuals and there was limited loyalty to it after Akhenaten's death.

After two or three years the king and his court left Amarna to return to the former royal capitals of Memphis and Thebes and to reinstate the traditional state gods. Tutankhaten and Ankhsenpaaten may have been personally reluctant to do this as they had both grown up at Amarna knowing no other cult than that of the Aten. However, there was no choice.

To emphasise the return to orthodoxy, the *Aten* element in both names was replaced by *Amun* (figure 12). Tutankh*amun* with Ankhsen*amun* reverted to the traditional roles of an Eighteenth Dynasty Pharaoh and his consort.

Memphis had retained its importance as the administrative centre of Egypt during the reign of Akhenaten. It now became the political capital and royal residence, while Thebes regained its position as religious centre for the state god, Amun (figure 13). General Horemheb, acting as King's Deputy and Regent, controlled political and military affairs from Memphis while Ay, the vizier, was in close personal attendance on the king and responsible for religious matters. When the royal presence was required at religious festivals Tutankhamun and his court moved to Thebes, returning to Memphis to carry out his political role. He used the lavishly decorated palace of Amenhotep III at Malkata in West Thebes and the palace of Tuthmosis I at Memphis.

To implement the return to orthodox religion, a vigorous programme of temple building was begun (figure 14). Akhenaten's abandonment of traditional gods had resulted in their temples falling into ruin and their estates being neglected. The Restoration Stela describes how Tutankhamun rebuilt the temples, embellishing them with richly decorated images of their gods, and reinstated endowments for their support, especially the temples of Amun at Thebes and the temple of Ptah at Memphis. This activity was the visible evidence that the old order was restored, with a strong administration in control. Once again there was employment for the labour force attached to temples and temple estates, and the people were no longer excluded from state religion. When images of Amun and other gods were carried in procession through the streets and transported by barge along the canals, the crowds could participate in the divine presence and request oracular judgements from the gods for their problems. For example, detailed reliefs at Luxor Temple show the reinstated Festival of Opet (figure 15), which previously had been celebrated

15. Soldiers marching quickly with standards, shields, spears and clubs in procession for the Festival of Opet, Luxor Temple colonnade. (Photograph by Frances Welsh.)
16. Sandstone columns at Luxor Temple built by Amenhotep III: closed-papyrus bundles and open-papyrus colonnade, the walls decorated by Tutankhamun with scenes of procession for the Festival of Opet. (Photograph by Frances Welsh.)

annually in the second month of Inundation (July) at least from the early Eighteenth Dynasty. At Luxor a relief shows Tutankhamun offering *maat* to Amun to symbolise the return of divine order to Egypt as described in the Restoration Stela.

The consolations offered to the living by Amun were matched by those offered to the dead by the revived cult of Osiris. The Aten doctrine had seemed to revert to Old Kingdom beliefs and offered no hope to non-royal people for an afterlife except in the service of Pharaoh, whereas the Osiris cult had encouraged them to hope for personal salvation.

The traditional concepts of kingship were revived and the internal administration was strengthened and reorganised. Under the leadership of Ay and Horemheb official posts were filled by men loyal to Tutankhamun and committed to the restoration of Amun. These included Maya, as Chief Treasurer and Controller of Works, Usermont and Pentu, as viziers of north and south, Nakhtmin as Commander of the Army of Upper Egypt and Parannefer as High Priest of Amun. Lesser official posts were filled by members of noble families who were known and respected in their local communities.

To confirm this return to orthodoxy, Tutankhamun stressed his direct relationship with Amenhotep III by resuming work at temples founded by him or building on nearby sites. The colonnade of Luxor Temple was completed and its walls were decorated (figure 16). At Karnak additions, including a small temple, were made to the Temple of Amun and the approach to the Temple of Mut was lined with ram-headed sphinxes. A tomb was prepared for the king in the Western Valley at Thebes, near that of Amenhotep III, and a mortuary temple was planned.

In Nubia, Tutankhamun completed Amenhotep III's temple at Soleb and built temples for his own divine cult at Faras and Kawa to indicate that a traditional Pharaoh had regained control of Egypt. This may have followed a short military campaign, after which the administration of Nubia was centred at the towns of Faras and Soleb. Tutankhamun appointed Huya as Viceroy of Nubia and King's Son of Kush. With support from Egyptianised Nubian princes, he controlled the import of African goods and ensured a steady supply of gold and other valuable commodities (figure 17). Trade with the Levant and the eastern Mediterranean continued and Egyptian influence was reinforced by a show of military strength in southern Palestine led by Horemheb. Deputations from Palestine and Nubia came to Egypt to assure Tutankhamun of their loyalty and their wish to continue trading.

17. Tribute presented by Egyptianised Nubians to the Viceroy of Kush under Tutankhamun; painted scene in Theban tomb no. 40 Huya. (Photograph by Frances Welsh.)

Great wealth flowed into Egypt, internal divisions were healed and popular discontent satisfied. The young king was expected to establish a new royal blood line, but his death in Year 10 of his reign ended such hopes. The cause of his death is not certain. It is unlikely to have been assassination, but it was a totally unexpected event. His tomb was not completed and the grave goods and funerary equipment for him had not been fully prepared. There was no royal heir except Ankhsenamun, who could not be considered suitable because she was Akhenaten's daughter.

In the event, Ay took control and buried Tutankhamun with some hastily assembled funerary equipment in a makeshift tomb in the burial place of his ancestors, the Valley of the Kings at Thebes.

3

The significance of Tutankhamun's tomb

Tutankhamun's tomb elucidates various aspects of his contemporary history and culture. Although little is new or unique in the tomb, its contents are significant for interpreting evidence available from other sources.

The location of the tomb

Tutankhamun was buried in a tomb of modest size cut into the lowest level of the floor of the Valley of the Kings at Thebes. Earlier Eighteenth Dynasty royal burials were in hidden locations at the ends of the side branches of the Valley, but this tomb was in a central position (figure 2).

His immediate predecessors had not chosen to be buried in this valley: Akhenaten prepared the Royal Tomb at Amarna for himself and his family and the tomb of Amenhotep III (WV22) was in the Western Valley at Thebes. Two further tombs were being prepared in the Western Valley, one of which (WV23) was subsequently used by Ay, Tutankhamun's successor.

The indications of hasty preparation, the non-royal features of the wall decorations and the small size of Tutankhamun's tomb (KV62) may imply that Ay had originally prepared it for his own use. Tutankhamun's unexpected death gave Ay the opportunity to use it for the king and enabled him later to appropriate for his own use the tomb in the Western Valley intended for Tutankhamun. This could explain why, after his short reign of less than four years, Ay occupied a more completely decorated and larger tomb than did Tutankhamun, who reigned for ten years.

Whichever was the intended tomb, the locations of both confirm that the religious capital of Egypt was once again at Thebes as royal burials were again placed in the Theban necropolis.

The size and layout of the tomb are similar to that of Yuya and Thuya (KV46), the parents of Queen Tiye, who were granted a site in the royal valley. Amenhotep III may have decided to inaugurate the Western Valley as a new royal burial area because the hidden sites in the Eastern Valley had been filled. If that were the case, non-royal burials could be permitted there as they were separated from the royal necropolis. Ay may have been granted a similar honour in recognition of his high position as vizier and his close relationship with the royal family.

18. Model of fully rigged state boat with painted hull and other boats heaped behind, as found in the Treasury. (Courtesy of the Griffith Institute, Oxford.)

The preparation by Tutankhamun of a tomb in the Western Valley close to that of Amenhotep III confirms his desire to claim direct descent from him. That tomb is laid out with the straight axis introduced by Akhenaten, whereas the tomb he finally occupied in the Valley of the Kings has the curved axis of the earlier Eighteenth Dynasty tradition. Although small, the plan seems to have been adapted to conform with traditional royal burials by the provision of a sunken burial chamber with an adjacent storage room.

Historical information

Even though the tomb contained no written records it is historically informative because the identity of the body is not disputed. Tutankhamun's name in cartouches appears many times on objects placed upon the body and within the sealed burial chamber. The painted scene on the north wall of the burial chamber shows Pharaoh, God's Father Ay, performing the Osiride funerary rite for his predecessor, Tutankhamun (figure 19). Although older than Tutankhamun, Ay acts as Horus, the dutiful son and heir, in ensuring a proper burial for his father Osiris (in the person of Tutankhamun) in order to inherit the throne. The unprecedented inclusion of such a scene indicates Ay's lack of normal rights to the throne and also confirms the historical order of the two reigns. The probable length of Tutankhamun's reign is established by dates on wine jars in the tomb, Years 9 and 10 being the highest.

19. Ay performs the Opening of the Mouth ceremony on the shrouded mummy of Tutankhamun, who is then greeted by the goddess Nut on the left; painting on the north wall of the Burial Chamber. (Photograph by Frances Welsh.)

Although there are conflicting views on the exact age of the body, it is agreed that the last surviving male heir of the Eighteenth Dynasty was young at his accession. That his reign was a transition period between the Eighteenth and Nineteenth Dynasties is shown by objects in the tomb which demonstrate a clear sequence of change within Tutankhamun's reign. For example, the scene on the golden throne (figure 22) includes the Aten sundisk with rays extending over the royal couple, who are depicted in Amarna style, whereas the pectoral on Tutankhamun's corselet (figure 38) shows him in traditional dress and pose and accompanied by the restored state gods.

Tutankhamun's marriage to Ankhsenamun is confirmed by scenes depicted on the throne and golden shrine. His loyalty to Akhenaten's family is indicated by objects bearing their names, showing that the Aten was not desecrated in Tutankhamun's reign. Some objects in the tomb appear to have been prepared for the burials of other members of the Amarna royal family. Modern research techniques reveal that the name on some objects in the tomb was altered to that of Tutankhamun. The original name is sometimes Akhenaten but most often it is Ankheperure-Neferneferuaten, the name proposed for Nefertiti's kingly role. The name Smenkhkare Djoserkhepru does not appear. The second coffin, canopic coffinettes and some statuettes seem to be portraits of an individual who is not

20. Kiosk-shaped pectoral of gold inlaid with coloured glass with Wadjet, cobra goddess of Lower Egypt, and Nekhbet, vulture goddess of Upper Egypt, protecting Tutankhamun as Osiris. (Cairo Museum; Carter 261.o. Photograph by Frances Welsh.)

21. Royal diadem with removable cobra and vulture heads from the head of the mummy; gold inlaid with glass and semi-precious stones. (Cairo Museum; Carter 256.4.o. Photograph courtesy of Peter Clayton.)

Tutankhamun and some statuettes may represent a queen. These changes and appropriations may reflect the unexpectedly early death of Tutankhamun and may provide evidence for assessing the identity and role of the body in tomb KV55 (see page 8). It has been suggested that this is either Akhenaten or Smenkhkare, whose burials were brought to Thebes when Tutankhamun decided to re-inter his Amarna relatives near his newly established capital. The removal of the original hieroglyphic inscriptions from the outer surface of his sarcophagus may also be significant.

Tutankhamun's tomb clearly shows a return to the beliefs of the early Eighteenth Dynasty. The king is shown as a god, consorting with gods, but a priest must officiate at his funerary rites to ensure his survival in the afterlife. The cults of Amun and Osiris are fully re-established and traditional concepts of kingship restored (figure 20). The observance of Osiride funerary rites is stressed throughout. Amun replaced the Aten, not only in the king's name but also in the iconography. The pantheon of traditional gods is present and models of these, including Ptah, Nefertum and Sekhmet, accompany Tutankhamun. The vulture Nekhbet and the scarab beetle Khepri, which were not favoured by Akhenaten, are shown prominently on Tutankhamun's jewellery. The full royal regalia of a traditional king, including a variety of crowns, are depicted in paintings and on objects in the tomb, and the mummy wore a gold diadem (figure 21). Tutankhamun's royal crook and flail were found in the Antechamber.

The king's role as successful warrior and hunter is depicted in painted scenes on the sides and lid of a wooden casket (figure 55) and is stressed by the large collection of weapons and the epithets decorating them.

His divinity is expressed by giving each god the facial features of the king and depicting him as equal in size and status to the gods. The insignia on his forehead represent the cobra goddess Wadjet and the vulture goddess Nekhbet, the protectors of royalty, and these are repeated in the form of gold collars and models as well as in motifs on jewellery placed on his body. Tutankhamun's transformation into Osiris, King of the Dead, was completed by placing the full royal regalia upon his body with the crook, flail and uraei on the coffins and mask.

The concept of the king as dispenser of justice and upholder of *maat*, or perfect balance and order in the living world, is included in the inscriptions on the second shrine.

The reduction of the political role of the queen following the return to orthodoxy is apparent. On the golden throne, in Amarna style, she is of equal size to the king and receives the divine benefits of the Aten. The small golden shrine shows her earlier role of supporting him in his royal duties, while later objects do not show her. The sarcophagus and canopic shrine are protected by four funerary goddesses, whereas at Amarna it is the queen who protects the royal sarcophagus.

Archaeological perspectives

The undamaged condition of the objects and the completeness of the burial equipment provide a good corpus of material for archaeologists to clarify questions raised by incomplete evidence from other sites. Some objects, such as gloves, had not been found previously. The group of thirty-five boat models (figure 18) is unique and shows not only the design and proportional size of boats in the royal flotilla but also that these continued to be necessary inclusions in burial equipment. The unprecedented survival of six complete chariots with their harness provides information on how they were made and assembled, which cannot be deduced accurately from pictorial representations. Features that have been clarified include the position of the arrow holder, the check rowels and the hawk figure with a disk on its head placed on the yoke bar to face forward. Rare items from the Aten heresy period, such as the golden throne (figure 22), show that the transmission of technical and artistic skills from the early Eighteenth Dynasty was not disturbed by political changes.

The great number and variety of manufactured goods deposited in the tomb provides an invaluable opportunity to assess the skill and

22. The golden throne with cartouches of Tutankh*aten* and of Tutankh*amun*. On the backrest, Ankhsenamun anoints Tutankhamun beneath the rays of the Aten disk. The matching footstool has six figures of Egypt's traditional enemies. See figures 12 and 30. (Cairo Museum; Carter 91. Photograph courtesy of Peter Clayton.)

technological ability of craftsmen in Egypt in the late Eighteenth Dynasty. Carpentry, stoneworking and metalworking techniques, as well as the methods used for textile making and leatherwork, can be studied in detail. The excellent quality of craftsmanship indicates that high standards were maintained through the Amarna period and into Tutankhamun's reign by the craftsmen of the royal workshops, who probably accompanied the court each time it moved to a new location.

Above all, the undisturbed layout in the Burial Chamber and Treasury, which was carefully recorded during excavation, offers unique evidence for Egyptian religious beliefs and burial practices. All other royal burials from the New Kingdom were disturbed and robbed in antiquity, leaving scattered objects whose original position was uncertain. Here, the guardian figures were found, as they had

23. Model of Tutankhamun wearing the Red Crown of Lower Egypt and a long Amarna kilt, standing on a papyrus skiff poised to harpoon the hippopotamus representing evil forces, as Horus conquering Seth; gold leaf over wood, draped with linen as found. (From Carter, *The Tomb of Tutankhamun*, volume 3, 1933, plate XIII. Courtesy of the Griffith Institute, Oxford.)

been placed, at the entrance to the burial chamber, the four magical bricks and statuettes in their places, the sealed funerary shrines in correct sequence with symbolic objects suitably placed. Only an undisturbed tomb could yield details such as the draping of linen cloths over most of the statuettes (figure 23); the presence and position of the linen canopy studded with golden rosettes, which shaded the third shrine; the use of the scarab motif so extensively in Tutankhamun's jewellery; the placing of wreaths of fresh flowers on the brow and neck of each coffin; the attachment, at this early date, of the *ba* bird amulet to the chest of the shrouded body. Finally, the mummy itself demonstrated the ritual sequence of bandaging and the arrangement of amulets and jewellery required for a royal burial.

As techniques improve, it is possible that the tomb may provide new clues about Tutankhamun's parents and the identity of Smenkhkare. The significance of the small golden shrine and the Weret-Hekau amulet within it (figure 24) is not fully understood but this, and items previously unknown, such as the portable canopy, the T-shaped amulet and obscure funerary emblems (see below), provide useful references of known provenance.

Tutankhamun's place in the archaeological sequence leading from the Eighteenth to the Nineteenth Dynasty is settled. The style of his stone sarcophagus links Akhenaten with Horemheb and the nature and arrangement of the funerary equipment foreshadows that shown on the tomb walls of Nineteenth and Twentieth Dynasty kings, as, for example, in the earliest known example of the text of the Book of the Divine Cow, which is inscribed on the outer shrine.

24. Amulet of the snake goddess Weret-Hekau suckling the king; of sheet gold over a core, from the golden shrine in the Treasury. (Cairo Museum; Carter 108.c. Photograph by Frances Welsh.)

4

The Pharaoh's life

It appears that the luxurious lifestyle of Eighteenth Dynasty royalty continued to be enjoyed by Tutankhamun.

Resources and technology

The contents of the tomb show the wide range of materials available, both imported and locally produced. The use of some items of burial equipment which had been intended for another individual seems to result from unpreparedness rather than a scarcity of materials. Flax for textiles, wood for small objects, calcite, natron, some semi-precious stones and some gold were all available within Egypt. Imported materials included silver, copper, perfumed oils and lapis lazuli, which came via the Levant, and turquoise and copper from Sinai. Gold, together with African ivory, ebony, ostrich feathers, animal skins and incense came from Nubia and the south.

There were many wooden objects in the tomb. The skilfully carved lifelike figures of gods and sacred animals show complete mastery of wood carving (figure 26) and these carved statues were coated with a thin layer of plaster made of whiting and glue, called gesso. This was painted with a matt black varnish of resin on to which gold leaf was glued to cover the statue or highlight certain features. The statuettes of anthropoid gods and goddesses are fully overlaid with gold leaf, whereas animal figures such as the Anubis jackal and the black leopard have face markings of gold. The two life-size guardian figures have gold on their kilts and royal insignia. Good-quality close-grained wood was left uncovered, as in the shabtis with unpainted faces and the model of Osiris given by Maya, Overseer of the Treasury.

Mortice and tenon joints and dovetail joints were used in carpentry and wooden elements of chariots, stools and boxes were glued and dowelled to give additional strength. Dowels were usually capped and hidden within the decorative designs of chairs and beds. Poor-quality local wood was skilfully masked and decorated attractively using various materials and techniques. One box is veneered with a thin sheet of wood, but the usual method of decoration was with marquetry or complicated inlays of wood, ivory, semi-precious stones, coloured glass and faience. Silver was used to enrich the inlaid scene on the back of the throne and bark was used to decorate weapons.

25. Funerary portrait mask of Tutankhamun; of sheet gold beaten and inlaid with lapis lazuli, faience and coloured glass. See figures 27 and 51. (Cairo Museum; Carter 256. a. Photograph by Frances Welsh.)

26. (Left) Model of Tutankhamun wearing the White Crown of Upper Egypt, with flail and staff; gold leaf on wood, from the Treasury. (Cairo Museum; Carter 256.b. Photograph courtesy of Peter Clayton.)
27. (Right) The gold mask of Tutankhamun (rear view). See figures 25 and 51. (Cairo Museum; Carter 256.a. Photograph by Frances Welsh.)

Metal objects in the tomb confirm the skill of the metalworkers and the variety of their techniques, including the processes of annealing, soldering and 'lost-wax' casting. Decoration was produced by hammering, engraving and polishing, and jewellery was embellished with repoussé work, chasing and granulation. The unique rose-purple colour of some small gold items was caused by traces of iron in the ore used and may have been produced unintentionally. Tools and weapons were made of copper and bronze, as were components of horse harness. Complicated hinges were used on the folding bed and on several boxes.

The two outer coffins and the gold throne are of wood covered with thin sheet gold, whereas the innermost coffin and gold mask are of sheet gold beaten into shape and burnished to a high polish (figures 25 and 27). Inlays of semi-precious stones, glass and faience are fixed into spaces made for them. Pectorals and pendants were decorated with motifs modelled in gold cloisonné filled with cut inlays. These were suspended either on gold wire, twisted or plaited, or on flexible straps formed by stringing together plaques and beads of various sizes and materials.

Gold, copper and bronze were extensively used. Silver is rare and usually occurs in small quantities. The ceremonial dagger with gold blade shows the highest technical skill and may have been a diplomatic gift. The matching dagger with a blade of iron is an exceptional item and was probably imported. The sixteen small chisel blades of iron in the tomb were probably produced locally by hammering. The small headrest amulet of iron seems to have been inexpertly made, perhaps in Egypt, but the origin of the iron amuletic eye set into a gold bracelet is unknown. The small number and symbolic nature of the items made of iron confirm that Egypt was still a Bronze Age culture.

Stone vessels in the tomb are of the high technical and artistic

28. Translucent calcite lamp with a scene of the royal couple painted between its double walls and visible only when lit. (From Carter, *The Tomb of Tutankhamen*, volume 2, 1927, plate XLVI. Courtesy of the Griffith Institute, Oxford.)

standard shown by the stone statues of the period. Made of calcite (Egyptian alabaster), their elaborate designs demonstrate a complete mastery of stoneworking. The translucent quality of the calcite is exploited, especially in one lamp where decoration on the outer surface of the inner stone lining is visible only when lit from within (figure 28). Glass and faience were used to make storage jars for oils and perfumes as well as for decorative inlays. The vulture pectoral may represent the earliest known example of enamelling.

A large amount of linen material was found in the tomb. The skill and innovative abilities of textile workers are demonstrated by examples of linen weaving which range in quality from gossamer-thin muslin to coarse woven cloth and there are two fragments of rare embroidered tapestry work (chariot harness). Fine stitching is visible on the seams of the child's shirt and tunics, and woven or embroidered bands of pattern decorate the ceremonial robe. Tapestry-woven motifs decorate gloves, a bag and a quiver. Appliqués of metal or leather and woven plaques were added to robes.

The weapons and chariots are the work of technically competent craftsmen in woodwork, metallurgy and decoration with inlays, including coloured barks.

The function of the whole tomb and its contents was to achieve a safe and happy afterlife for Tutankhamun. Each item was included for a specific purpose and had special significance as a component part of the whole. Provision was made for every practical aspect of the king's daily life after death, and for both his spiritual and physical survival.

The objects in the tomb fit broadly into two categories: those of a type used in life, and those of a type for use solely after death. Items of a type used in life predominated in the Antechamber and Annexe and were separated from the burial.

Objects used in life

These items ensured that the dead king would continue to live in the physical comfort he had enjoyed while alive. Although Egyptians believed that the dead king became Osiris and was received into the company of gods after death, they retained the belief that he would continue to have human needs. Hence the inclusion of furniture with accessories and equipment for personal and ceremonial use as well as ample provision of food and drink. The earthly quality of the dead king's continued existence is depicted in the scenes on the small golden shrine. Tutankhamun and his queen enjoy the pleasures and activities of mortal life and use furniture, equipment and clothing similar to that included in the tomb (figure 10).

The palace furnishings

The assemblage of furniture – chairs, stools, beds and storage chests (figure 29) – together with accessories and personal equipment constitute the furnishings of a small palace. Many were well made and richly decorated with inscriptions and decorative scenes indicating close personal associations with Tutankhamun and Ankhsenamun. Each category includes a variety of designs with different functions and the objects do not appear to have been made especially for the burial.

Six chairs and twelve stools without backrests were included and a wide low-backed seat 24.2 cm high for a young child. The

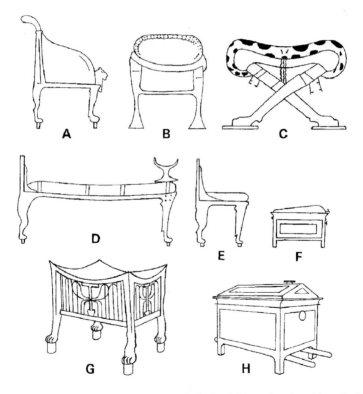

29. Eighteenth Dynasty furniture: A, armchair; B, rigid stool and cushion; C, folding stool with feline foot finials to crossed legs and oxhide seat; D, bed, mattress and headrest; E, chair; F, chest inlaid with ivory and ebony; G, Tutankhamun's rigid stool with feline legs, double coved seat, braces in *sma-tawy* design of white-painted wood; H, Tutankhamun's large funerary chest with retractable carrying poles, of ebony with inlaid inscriptions. (Cairo Museum. Drawings by R. B. Welsh.)

30. Golden
throne (rear view)
showing uraei frieze
and supports for
chair back-rest with
Tutankh*aten* and
Ankhsenpa*aten* in
cartouches. See
figures 12 and 22.
(Cairo Museum;
Carter 91. Photograph
by Frances Welsh.)

armchair for an older child is of conventional design and made of
ebony with fine ivory inlay decoration. Each of the five full-size
chairs is of different materials, design and decoration and each
probably served a different function. Divine figures and hieroglyphic
inscriptions decorate the vertical surfaces and the symbols of
unity, the *sma-tawy,* to represent the union of the Two Lands, are
incorporated into the supporting struts and braces between the legs.
The back of each is supported by three vertical braces and the seat
is usually deeply coved. The chairs usually have leonine legs with
paws supported on circular drums. All are of wood except for one
made of papyrus.

An armless chair of deep red wood has a fine carving of the
kneeling god Heh to symbolise a reign of thousands of years, and a
low white-painted chair has on its back an open design of a falcon

with crook wings as divine protector of the king.

Two of the chairs may be thrones. These appear to have been made early in the reign as both the 'Aten' and 'Amun' forms of the king's name appear on them.

The magnificent golden throne is an armchair with extensive decorative detail including two carved lion heads forming capitals to the front legs. The armrests have openwork carving of the crowned cobra goddess Wadjet, whose wings protect the cartouches. A row of rearing cobras decorates the back, and the supporting struts and braces carry further symbolic decoration (figure 30). The throne backrest has an elaborate scene in relief of Tutankhamun and Ankhsenamun beneath the sundisk, fashioned from semi-precious stones, faience, coloured glass and silver, all set into a background of sheet gold. Sheet gold with an inlaid design covers the flat seat.

In contrast, the 'ecclesiastical' throne is a folding stool with crossed legs made rigid by the addition of two long rails supporting a tall

31. 'Ecclesiastical' throne with Tutankh*aten* and Tutankh*amun* in cartouches on the backrest; ebony covered with gold foil and inlaid with ivory, glass, faience and coloured stones. The matching footstool has nine figures of Syrian and Nubian enemies; from the Annexe. (Cairo Museum, Carter 351 and 378. Photograph by Frances Welsh.)

backrest (figure 31). The intricate designs are inlaid with precious materials. Each throne has a matching footstool with inlaid figures representing Egypt's prostrate enemies in Syria and Nubia. Eight additional footstools and four beaded hassocks were provided.

The twelve stools include two folding stools with duckhead finials to crossed legs connected by base rails and having oxhide seats. A third stool of similar design has a rigid seat inlaid with ivory to imitate animal skin markings and a wooden 'tail' hanging behind. Most of the stools are of the simple straight-legged form with a double-coved seat and vertical and diagonal braces between the legs. Two have lion legs and openwork grilles in the *sma-tawy* design. An unusual white-painted stool has three legs arranged as a tripod under a semicircular seat. The legs are canine and the seat is finely carved to show two lions bound head to tail by their feet. A running spiral pattern decorates the edge of the seat.

No cushions or decorative draperies were found except for a goose-feather filled cushion which is associated with a small rectangular stool. This has bronze staples for leather carrying straps and may form part of the king's travelling equipment with the two wooden panniers, the large portable chest with retractable poles, and the portable canopy and folding bed.

The lightweight folding bed is a unique survival. Two extra pairs of legs support the frame, which is divided into three sections by intricate copper hinges which enable the flexible woven mattress to be folded into a Z-shape. Like the five other beds, it is of conventional design: a rectangular wooden frame with a mattress of woven linen thread and a rectangular footboard standing on short leonine legs. Two curved stretchers to support the body weight are usually placed beneath the mattress of the beds.

One luxurious bed, showing signs of use, had the frame and the footboard covered with gold sheet 3.5 mm thick, fixed in place with small gold-topped pegs and decorated with an heraldic design of papyrus and lotus plants. Two others are partly gilded. Their footboards are decorated with the household gods, Bes and Taurt.

Linen stolen from the tomb probably included bed coverings. Eight full-sized headrests were found, six being of simple waisted type, one made of turquoise blue glass and another of deep blue faience. One ivory headrest is a unique variant of the waisted type. It represents the Egyptian view of the cosmos, as Shu, god of the atmosphere, with his upraised arms supporting the curving heaven, kneels between the recumbent lions of the Two Horizons. Another ivory headrest resembles a folding stool with duckhead finials. Its flexible 'pillow' has masks of Bes at each end to protect the sleeper.

32. Cedar-wood box inlaid with ivory and decorated with gilded wood symbols for life and dominion, and with names and titles of Tutankhamun and Ankhsenamun, with sixteen compartments inside, from the Treasury. (Cairo Museum; Carter 271. Photograph by Frances Welsh.)

Belongings were kept in chests or caskets which were both functional and decorative. Most of those provided for Tutankhamun are single unique examples whose functions are indicated by their contents, the hieratic labels attached and the quality of material and decoration. Apart from special boxes containing food, shabtis and divine emblems, there were over fifty chests for storage. Most are rectangular but four are cartouche-shaped and one is bow-fronted. Lids are vaulted, flat, gabled or sloping and most have a projecting knob which matches a similar knob on the end of the box. This arrangement enabled a seal to be placed on a cord wound from one knob to the other. Some lids are hinged and one has an additional inner lid. Where required, the interior space is divided by vertical boards into six, eight or more sections (figure 32). One has a mushroom-shaped fitting to support a crown or wig, and a small box used by Tutankhamun in childhood is fitted with numerous hinged and sliding inner lids and compartments. Unique locking devices are used on two boxes. Three are fixed on tall legs strengthened with bracing struts and grilles similar to those on stools.

The wooden chests are decorated with inlaid designs of ivory, gold, faience, semi-precious stones or wood marquetry. One of them has painted scenes of the king in his chariot. Other materials used include calcite (a casket with vaulted lid), gold (an openwork lid) and papyrus reed (a box lined with linen).

Undecorated white-painted chests contained mundane items such as underlinen, while jewellery, embroidered linen robes and precious items were stored in richly decorated caskets, such as the one with blue faience and gold inlays containing priestly robes, the royal sceptre and jewellery. Walking sticks and bows and arrows were kept in a long ebony box with a hinged lid.

Dried food was stored in more than 116 round, oval or bottle-shaped baskets. Many had lids and one took the form of a round serving dish with partitions. Vessels of calcite, metal, faience and glass were used to store oils and fats, and pottery jars were used for wine and honey.

Elaborate decorative pieces carved from translucent calcite were presumably for display as ornaments. These combine beauty with practical purpose as lamps or as containers for oil and perfumed unguents, although the purpose of the ibex-headed boat with a crew of two girl dwarfs flanking a small shrine is uncertain.

The public and personal equipment of the Pharaoh

The concept of divine kingship in the Eighteenth Dynasty was expressed by the image which Pharaoh presented to his people. Special regalia and clothing emphasised his unique position of power, and his personal vigour and ability to rule were demonstrated by his skills with weapons and chariotry. Processions on land and water on civil and religious occasions displayed the royal power and magnificence to the people and reinforced their loyalty.

As Tutankhamun expected to continue this role in his life after death, suitable equipment was included: richly decorated ceremonial fans and staves, and musical instruments to be carried by courtiers escorting the king in his gold-covered state chariot or royal barge; working chariots and weapons for his military and sporting use; ceremonial robes, including leopardskin cloaks, for his duties as High Priest for all the gods of Egypt.

Full royal regalia were provided within the Burial Chamber, where the king became Osiris, and there were two additional sets of the crook and flail with an *aba* sceptre in the Antechamber. The gold diadem on the mummy was the only royal crown found.

The six chariots with accessories were designed to serve separate functions. All are light chariots to be drawn by two horses and are constructed of bent wood and leather with six-spoked wheels.

33. Flotilla of boats of the Viceroy of Nubia, including ceremonial barges and work boats; painted scene in Theban tomb no. 40 Huya. (Photograph by Frances Welsh.)

They are full size and appear to have been used. The first state processional chariot is overlaid with gold sheet and patterned in alternate bands of embossed relief and inlaid coloured glass and stones. The second state chariot is also covered with gold leaf. Its relief decoration includes a depiction of bound captives of various racial types on the cabin interior. The other four are plain hunting chariots. Sufficient harness and accessories were included.

The collection of thirty-five wooden model boats includes funerary boats but also appears to represent three complete flotillas for processions by water. Three large fully rigged sailing ships with double steering oars at the rear resemble the Viceroy's state ship with brightly decorated hull and cabin shown in the tomb of Huya (figure 33). The boats and barges clustering around the Pharaoh's state barge in the Festival of Opet relief in Luxor Temple are represented by eight barges with double steering oars and sixteen single-oared working boats suitable for cargo, transport, fishing and cooking.

Attendant courtiers are indicated by seven ostrich-feather fans, decorated with gold and inlays, which have long handles for ceremonial

34. Musicians with lutes and clappers followed by men clapping hands rhythmically in procession at the Festival of Opet, Luxor Temple. (Photograph by Frances Welsh.)

use. Two state trumpets of silver and copper alloy, ivory clappers and a pair of sistra complete this group (figure 34).

The king would have worn fine clothing enhanced by richly decorated accessories, which included an ostrich-feather fan with an L-shaped handle of ivory, for personal use. This fan was the only one on which original feathers are preserved. There was also a choice of numerous decorated staves for him to carry: most were mounted in gold and silver with patterned bands of semi-precious stones and inlaid barks. One of gold and another of silver may have been carried in the coronation procession as each is topped with a small standing statue of the king. The curved crooks of four staves are modelled to represent captives bound ankle to ankle.

The group of about 130 sticks includes hunting and fighting sticks, and a full range of weapons was provided: bows and arrows, swords (including two scimitars), slings, throwsticks and boomerangs, together with eight shields and a protective leather tunic. Two gold-mounted daggers were placed on the king's body.

The importance of the king's role as successful warrior is demonstrated by the provision of chariots, composite bows and scimitars, which symbolised the Eighteenth Dynasty Pharaoh's control of north Syria, where the technology to make them had developed. Fourteen self-bows and at least 29 composite bows were provided, together with numerous arrows of various shapes and materials according to their use. The self-bows are ordinary long bows, whereas the composite or compound bows are more powerful weapons made of wood, horn and sinew held together with gum and bindings of bark or leather.

There were two scimitar-swords (*khepesh*), one full-size and one suitable for a child. The four ceremonial shields are gilded and have cut-out scenes of the victorious Pharaoh (figures 35 and 36). The four military shields are solid and covered with oxhide. Tutankhamun's body armour was a sleeveless linen bodice overlaid with rows of leather scales to protect the torso, while gloves and armguards of leather and fabric protected his hands and arms.

Clothes include tunics, shirts, over a hundred triangular loincloths to be worn under a kilt and a selection of belts, scarves, shawls and capes. One ceremonial tunic of fine linen has woven bands of tapestry in bright colours and others sparkle with applied rosettes and beads of gold and semi-precious stones. There were twenty-seven linen gloves in the tomb, some in matching pairs, some with tapestry-woven decoration, and over ninety sandals made of leather, linen,

35. Ceremonial shield of gilded wood with an openwork design of Tutankhamun as a sphinx trampling Nubian enemies. (Cairo Museum; Carter 379.a. Photograph by Frances Welsh.)

36. Two ceremonial shields similar to those in the tomb, brought as tribute from Nubia. (After Davies and Gardiner, *Tomb of Huy No. 40*, 1926, plate XXV.)

37. Tutankhamun's sandals with Syrians and Nubians and Nine Bows on the inner sole to represent the Pharaoh's role in trampling on his enemies. Leather with marquetry veneer. (Cairo Museum; Carter 397. Photograph by Frances Welsh.)

38. Pectoral showing Tutankhamun before Amun-Re, followed by Atum and his consort Iusaas, on corselet of broad collar, pectoral and counterpoise, joined to the bodice with shoulder straps for a ceremonial garment of gold cloisonné and coloured inlays. (Cairo Museum. Carter 54.k. Photograph courtesy of Peter Clayton.)

papyrus or rush, again including matching pairs (figure 37).

Cosmetics and personal toilet equipment were provided: mirrors in decorative cases, razors, kohl tubes, cosmetic boxes. A set of bandages with a linen finger-stall was included.

On ceremonial occasions the king wore elaborate bead collars, suspended pectoral ornaments and bracelets. Tutankhamun's jewelled corselet combines the collar and pectoral in one garment (figure 38). Dockets listing the contents of boxes reveal that there had been an extensive range of jewellery. Most of it seems to have been stolen but other pieces remained on the intact burial or were overlooked (figure 39). These are mostly of gold inlaid with semi-precious stones, coloured glass, faience and lapis lazuli, and the designs incorporate divine symbols giving protection to the wearer. Among them were a large number of finger rings and sets of earrings and earstuds.

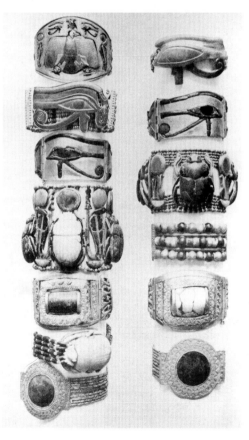

39. Bracelets found on the arms of Tutankhamun, six on the left and seven on the right, of amuletic designs including a rebus of Nebkheperure, in flexible beadwork of rigid hinged type; of gold, electrum, coloured stones and glass. (From Carter, *The Tomb of Tutankhamen*, volume 2, 1927, plate LXXXVI. Courtesy of the Griffith Institute, Oxford.)

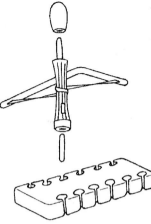

40. Tutankhamun's fire-making apparatus, which used a bow-drill and resin-lined firestock (bow not found). (Carter 585.aa. After Carter, *The Tomb of Tutankhamen*, volume 3, 1933, plate XXXVIII.)

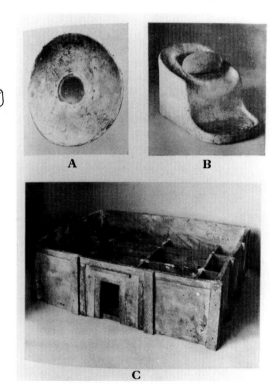

A

B

C

41. A, beer strainer of wood and copper; B, model of thrusting hand mill set into wooden frame with tray for flour; C, model granary, each section found filled with a different variety of grain. (From Carter, *The Tomb of Tutankhamen*, volume 3, 1933, plate LXV. Courtesy of the Griffith Institute, Oxford.)

Apart from small-scale furniture and weapons, youthful keepsakes include nearly fifty child's garments with patterned gloves, sandals, scarves and caps. The dockets on three boxes read: 'The equipment of his majesty when he was a child.' The casket fitted with multiple internal compartments and lids contained a childish collection of jewellery, a small gameboard, a pair of slings and a small bow-drill firelighter (figure 40). The young king's well-used writing equipment accompanied him as well as an ornately decorated royal set and boards with gaming pieces for the game of *senet*. A walking stick made of a plain reed set into a handle of gold was proudly inscribed: 'a reed which his majesty cut with his own hand' – presumably in youth. The young king's accession name of Tutankhaten appears on a small crook and flail, the emblems of royalty.

Items bearing the names of the members of the Amarna royal family may represent mementoes of his childhood: ivory writing palettes inscribed for Meritaten and Meketaten, a box lid of Neferneferure, ivory clappers of Meritaten, and a fan stock with Akhenaten's cartouches. Other items bearing royal names appear to be heirlooms.

Provision for the king's life in the tomb included a supply of food and drink: joints of meat in ovoid boxes, vegetables, fruits, edible seeds stored in baskets and stocks of stoned dates with two jars of honey for sweetness. Grains of barley and emmer wheat, an overflowing model granary, a model grinder (figure 41) and cooked loaves provided the staple Egyptian diet and the ingredients for making beer. There were more than thirty wine jars that had contained wine from a variety of royal vineyards. Dockets give the date of vintage, the location of the vineyard and the name of the vintner. It seems that the ancient Egyptians appreciated that pleasures which had enhanced Pharaoh's life on earth would be required in his life after death.

42. The east wall of the Burial Chamber with the entrance to the Treasury. The wall painting shows twelve palace officials wearing white mourning headbands pulling Tutankhamun's funerary sledge to the tomb. (Photograph by Frances Welsh.)

5

The Pharaoh in death

Tutankhamun's death was dealt with in the customary manner: the body was prepared in the traditional way, orthodox funerary rites were performed, and the burial was probably completed within the usual period of seventy days.

Funerary rites

To ensure his life after death, the king's body had to be preserved from physical decay. First the body was washed and purified, then soft tissue and internal organs were removed by way of a horizontal incision on the left side of the central abdomen. (In Tutankhamun's case the angle and position of this incision were unusual.) The brain was removed with a hook inserted through the nasal passage. The body was then desiccated in a bed of dry natron salts.

The desiccated body was carefully bandaged and wrapped to preserve its form, divine emblems and symbolic objects being placed between each layer of wrapping. The magical protection these provided was activated by recitations by the officiating priest.

The mummy was placed beneath a colourful canopy on a frame and transported upon a sledge pulled by twelve important members of the king's entourage (figure 42). A traditional funerary procession probably accompanied the hearse: bearers of equipment and offerings, professional mourning women and priests, personal friends and the grieving widow. Ay took the leading role as *sem*-priest.

The mummified body in its multi-layered cocoon of linen bandages and shrouds was then placed in the innermost coffin of a nest of three anthropoid coffins laid upon a low bed within the quartzite sarcophagus (figure 43). Wreaths and garlands of flowers were placed upon the brow and chest of each modelled portrait of the king while oils and resins were poured over each coffin (figure 44). Three gilded wooden shrines and a fine linen canopy spread over a frame and, lastly, the outermost gilded shrine were erected around the sarcophagus (figures 45 and 64).

The burial chamber was swept clean and the entrance blocked with a plastered wall. Then all the debris from the embalming, the funerary rituals and the funerary feast was placed in the unblocked entrance corridor before the entry was finally sealed.

Before it was unwrapped, Egyptologists had hoped that the body would be well preserved and could therefore provide information

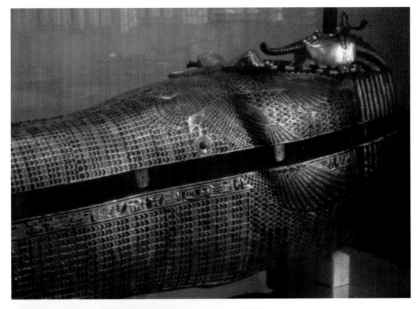

43. The second coffin of wood covered with gold foil and inlaid with faience, glass and semi-precious stones in a feather design, the lid attached by ten inscribed silver tenons held in place by gold-headed silver nails; probably made for Smenkhkare. (Cairo Museum; Carter 254. Photograph by Frances Welsh.)

44. The third coffin, as first revealed, with inlaid eyes and floral and bead collarettes; heavy gold sheet beaten to shape and burnished. (From Carter, *The Tomb of Tutankhamen*, volume 2, 1927, plate XXXVI. Courtesy of the Griffith Institute, Oxford.)

45. Diagrammatic section to show the arrangement of the four shrines and three coffins protecting the mummified body of Tutankhamun, resting on a low bed inside the quartzite sarcophagus. (Drawing by R. B. Welsh.)

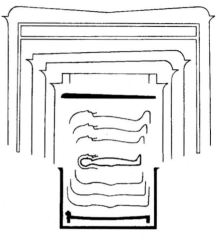

about the cause of the king's death, his age and who his parents were, but unfortunately overzealous embalming had caused damage. An identified body such as Tutankhamun's should be useful for establishing relationships with other royal bodies because modern techniques can enable physical data such as blood types and skull characteristics to be ascertained. However, this research has been hampered by lack of secure identification for some of the other royal mummies, which appear to have been labelled incorrectly when they were hastily reburied in safe caches by necropolis priests. From skull measurements it appears that Tutankhamun was related to the Eighteenth Dynasty royal family: skull characteristics are similar, especially the jaw line. These measurements also indicate that the mummy attributed to Tuthmosis IV is probably a direct ancestor of Tutankhamun's mummy, whereas that of Amenhotep III (if correctly attributed) cannot be his father or paternal grandfather.

X-rays reveal the close similarity of Tutankhamun's skull and the skull of the body in tomb KV55 and blood serum tests show that they were of the same blood group, although it is not a rare one. This could support the theory that they are either brothers, Smenkhkare and Tutankhamun, or father and son, Akhenaten and Tutankhamun.

Unfortunately the soft tissue of the mummy was extensively damaged by excessive application of funerary oils and resins, which has reduced the possibility of accurate DNA results. Carbonisation of the skeletal structure masked secure evidence for age at death. Estimates had varied between fifteen and twenty-seven years old but a CT scan examination revealed he was nineteen years old. There is no evidence for a partially healed blow to the head but visible damage to the left leg, which probably resulted in an infected flesh wound, suggests that death may have followed a fall from his chariot.

Objects for use after death

Items for use solely after death, including those required for funerary rituals, the burial furnishings and the equipment for the afterlife, were placed in the Burial Chamber and Treasury.

The dead king had to be protected from the perils of the Amduat (the underworld) as described in the Books of the Dead. Every potential danger had to be averted by a specific amulet or symbolic protection;

46. The canopic shrine of gilded wood containing the calcite canopic chest and protected by cobra friezes and four funerary goddesses, Isis, Nephthys, Neith and Selket. (Cairo Museum, Carter 266. Photograph by Frances Welsh.)

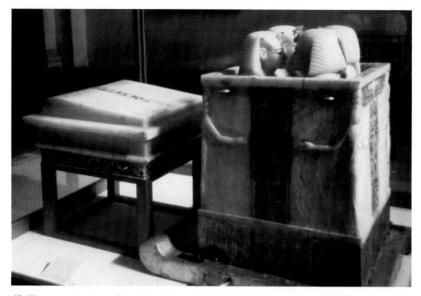

47. The canopic chest of banded calcite on the gilded wooden sledge, containing preserved viscera in four miniature coffins inside cavities with stoppers carved as portraits of Tutankhamun. (Cairo Museum; Carter 266.b. Photograph by Frances Welsh.)

every need had to be provided for. It is for this reason that such a vast quantity of goods, many of them apparently duplicated, was included. Every contingency was planned for, every danger anticipated, and multiple forms of protection were placed in the tomb.

Although a written papyrus roll may lie hidden within one of the wooden guardian figures, it appears that Tutankhamun relied for protection upon the permanent record of texts inscribed on the golden shrines and the solid manifestation of gods and protective symbols represented by wooden models placed around the burial.

The division between life and death was emphasised by the two statues guarding the blocked entrance to the Burial Chamber. Magical protective bricks and statuettes were inserted into niches in each wall of the Burial Chamber. The adjacent Treasury housed models of gods in shrines and model boats of a funerary nature. The canopic chest containing the king's mummified viscera, enclosed in multiple layers of protection similar to those used for the body, was also in the Treasury (figures 46 and 47).

The upper part of the body was shielded by the spreading wings of ten sheet-gold broad collars representing Wadjet (cobra), Nekhbet (vulture) and Horus (falcon). It was laden with jewelled pectorals and pendant necklaces as well as about twenty amulets suspended upon chains around the neck.

Additional broad collars, amuletic bracelets and gold circlets were placed on the body below the waist, where the two royal daggers were laid. Each forearm was covered from elbow to wrist with bracelets (figure 39) and the king's hands were protected by gold rings over sheet-gold finger-stalls. Sheet-gold toe-stalls and sandals of gold protected the feet. A skullcap with a beaded design protected the head (figure 48) beneath a linen coif on which was fixed the uraeus cobra in front and the sheet-gold vulture with outspread wings at the back. Above was the gold diadem and, finally, a circlet of cord supported the gold portrait mask.

The body received additional protection from its arrangement in the extended burial form of Osiris, the dead and resurrected king of Egypt. Osiris was traditionally represented as a bandaged mummy completely covered by a shroud from which his crowned head and two hands, crossed and holding royal sceptres, emerged. His face was always lifelike and clear of wrapping to indicate his rebirth. Tutankhamun's gold portrait mask, wearing the striped *nemes* headcloth, uraei and divine beard, was placed upon his shrouded body and two golden crossed hands holding the crook and flail were sewn to the cloth. The royal diadem was upon his head, the detachable royal insignia of cobra and vulture heads were nearby and, beneath the shroud, his waist was encircled by the regal girdle from which hung the beaded apron and bull's tail. Thus supernatural forces could recognise Tutankhamun as Osiris.

Although the dead king became Osiris he was required to make the perilous journey through the Amduat endured by non-royal Egyptians. Texts from the Books of the Dead setting out the dangers awaiting him and spells to surmount them were inscribed on the four golden shrines. Items required in rituals in the Underworld, such as the sacred oars, were placed around and between the shrines together with models of divine symbols, including the goose of Amun and the fetish of Anubis. Models of boats to carry the coffin to the sacred centres of Egypt, as well as solar barques for travel across the skies of the Underworld, were placed in the Treasury. The gods who would assist and protect Tutankhamun were placed there in the form of gilded models, some depicted carrying the king (figure 49), while gilded representations of the king performed rituals. He stands on a papyrus skiff harpooning the evil hippopotamus or is transported through dangerous places on the back of a black

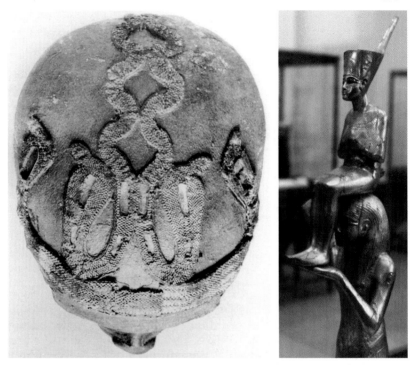

48. The head of Tutankhamun from above, wearing a beaded skullcap with a design of royal cobras including the cartouche of the Aten. (From Carter, *The Tomb of Tutankhamen*, volume 2, 1927, plate XXXII. Courtesy of the Griffith Institute, Oxford.)

49. Model of the goddess Menkheret carrying the king wearing the Red Crown; gilded wood. (Cairo Museum; Carter 296.a. Photograph courtesy of Peter Clayton.)

leopard. Hundreds of shabti figures were provided to carry out work he might be called upon to perform in the Fields of Iaru, together with numerous model hoes and agricultural tools.

An earth bed in the shape of Osiris and containing germinating barley was included to symbolise confidence in his final resurrection and, with this careful provision for every foreseeable physical and spiritual need, it seemed likely that this would be achieved.

6
Artistic styles in transition

Art in ancient Egypt had a useful function. Aesthetic considerations were subordinate to the practical purpose of providing funerary and religious requirements in a concrete form. Beliefs about the afterlife, as well as the political and divine aspects of kingship, required imperishable substitutes for the physical presence of people and offerings.

The types of materials used demonstrated Pharaoh's control of resources within Egypt and beyond its borders. The quality of craftsmanship indicated that he commanded skilled manpower. The style of art expressed and reinforced political and religious concepts. Changes in these concepts were manifested in changes in artistic styles. The reign of each Pharaoh was characterised by such changes, either subtle or emphatic.

Amarna style

It seems that Akhenaten made radical changes in art styles to signal the radical changes he was making in religious and political concepts. Tutankhamun's return to orthodoxy was signalled through the revival of traditional artistic styles. His need to be regarded as political successor of Amenhotep III could be emphasised by a reversion to the styles in art and architecture of that reign.

The style of the early Eighteenth Dynasty had been restrained but confident. Later, the luxurious lifestyle engendered by the influx of wealth from conquests was reflected in the increasingly elaborate art of Amenhotep III's reign. Amarna art exaggerated these themes: royal figures dressed in flowing robes of finely pleated transparent linen slouched on cushioned chairs; their children were portrayed playing in informal poses, while rows of courtiers bent from the waist. Akhenaten's own figure was shown in grotesque form, while the god was shown as the sundisk with extended arms as sun rays.

Once Akhenaten's regime was established, the extreme style was modified but the heavy jaw and long neck, with narrow-waisted large-hipped feminine body, were retained. Naturalistic rendering of flowers and animals reflected the influence of Aegean art styles. Animals were shown in the 'flying leap' pose where body and legs are stretched to full length and all feet are off the ground. Lively scenes of the activities of common people were included in temple and

50. (Left) Model of Isis in Amarna style and dress with a relief in traditional dress and wig on the canopic shrine; gilded wood. (Cairo Museum; Carter 266. Photograph by Frances Welsh.)
51. (Right) Profile of Tutankhamun's gold portrait mask. See figures 25 and 27. (Cairo Museum; Carter 256.a. Photograph courtesy of Peter Clayton.)

palace contexts, especially as crowds watching royal processions. Large figures of royalty dominated the mass of small, non-royal persons.

Tutankhamun's style

Influences from both the late Amarna Period and the reign of Amenhotep III can be seen in the artistic forms of Tutankhamun's reign, but a distinctive style finally emerged, as can be seen in the reliefs in the Luxor Temple (figure 53).

The wall paintings in Tutankhamun's tomb may reflect a delay in implementing changes in policy or show uncertainty on the part of the artists: whereas the proportions of the Ka figure on the north wall conform fully to the Amarna canon, on the south wall the canon of the earlier Eighteenth Dynasty is revived. However, all the figures have the full body and shorter leg of Amarna art, which was not finally abandoned in royal tomb art until the reign of Seti I.

Some objects in the tomb may have been made at Amarna. The golden throne displaying full Amarna iconography appears to have been completed before the Aten cult had been abandoned. Some of the wooden figures of goddesses and the king, and also some shabtis, may have been prepared for Amarna royal burials. Some of these display Amarna-type features but their restrained style makes it unlikely that they were stored at Thebes from the beginning of Akhenaten's reign, as has been suggested.

The scenes on the golden shrine show the king and queen in relaxed poses reminiscent of Amarna scenes, but their figures and faces have a slimmer appearance and the Aten is not present. The soft roundness of face and arms merely accentuates the extreme youth of the royal couple, as is evident in the two small figures of the king in silver and gold which stand on top of ceremonial staves and in the small squatting gold figure. This soft style was adopted as the distinctive feature of the young king for stone statues and reliefs depicting the reinstated cults of Amun and Osiris (figure 1). By the time of his death, he was portrayed as mature, with features more finely drawn, as on the ivory and ebony box. The golden mask is the supreme exemplar of this: the bone structure begins to show beneath the less chubby cheeks and nose and the full lips pout with adult sensuousness (figure 51). The shape of the face and features and the poise of the head upon the neck is similar to that of the small ebony head of Queen Tiye, thus accentuating her relationship, whether as mother or grandmother, to Tutankhamun. He is shown in this way in the reliefs on the back of the Second Pylon of Luxor Temple, which were carved late in the reign and usurped by Horemheb (figure 14).

The art style of Amenhotep III is revived in the finely carved representations of divine animals, such as the recumbent granite lion placed at Soleb Temple and the cow head of Hathor in the tomb. The small objects with carved animals may have originated in the Amarna workshops. The lion (figure 52), the ibex antelope or the duckling on its nest would not compromise Akhenaten's policy of disavowal of former gods.

The inclusion of flowers and vegetation in profusion continues the Amarna stress on naturalistic settings for royal scenes. The ivory and ebony box shows Tutankhamun and Ankhsenamun in a lush garden setting, holding garlands of flowers and leaves or shooting wild birds deep in a thicket of papyrus fronds.

52. Calcite ointment jar
with a royal lion on the
lid, a scene engraved on
the side of a lion attacking
a wild bull, and heads
of Nubian and Syrian
prisoners at the base;
knobs and lion's tongue
of ivory stained red. (Cairo
Museum; Carter 211.
Photograph courtesy of
Peter Clayton.)

The depiction here, and on the golden shrine, of the royal couple
alone together and equal in size continues the trend begun by
Amenhotep III. Queen Tiye was portrayed in this way in temples
and tombs, on reliefs and statues, as were the Amarna queens.
However, Ankhsenamun does not appear with Tutankhamun on the
Luxor reliefs and this anticipates the return to reduced prominence
for queens in official art.

The sense of movement and activity learned from Aegean art
is seen in the Festival of Opet reliefs. Whereas the king and the
sacred barque of Amun are depicted in formal static style, soldiers,
sailors and priests in the procession seem to move along the wall,
encouraged by lively onlookers and musicians accompanying
them. Bulls for sacrifice toss their heads (figure 53), Nubians and
Egyptians jostle in the crowd and, in the temple workrooms, cooks

53. Priests in elaborately pleated robes and sacrificial bulls with decorated horns welcome the image of Amun back to Karnak Temple; Festival of Opet relief at Luxor Temple. (Photograph by Frances Welsh.)

54. Preparation of food and offerings in booths at Luxor Temple for Amun's 'beautiful Festival of Opet'. (Photograph by Frances Welsh.)

busily prepare food and drink for the sacred offerings in scenes which recall Amarna tomb reliefs (figure 54). The decorated horns and deformed hooves of the sacrificial bulls are repeated in reliefs at Kawa Temple.

Scenes on the painted casket of Tutankhamun in his chariot show the development of hunting scenes from the early Eighteenth Dynasty, where the charioteer seems immobile but the fleeing animals leap above an undulating base line (Theban tomb no.108 Userhat). In a relief from Tuthmosis IV's chariot this became a mass of defeated chariots, horses and soldiers with no firm base line. Now, on this casket, in each scene a mass of animals or foreigners flees in haste from the arrows of the king and the flailing hooves of his horses (figure 55). Bodies twist and turn in the melée and there is no firm base line within it. A sense of forward movement is achieved as the king leans towards the horses. The use of space accentuates the ideological message. The king in his chariot has the strong visual support of a vertical row of charioteers at his back. His dominance is shown not only by his superior size and confident bearing but by the forward and upward movement of the bodies and front legs of the prancing horses. The remaining space is crammed with a mass of small figures offering no resistance to the mighty Egyptian Pharaoh. Antecedents such as these of Nineteenth Dynasty battle reliefs were presumably transmitted by other examples on boxes or papyrus rolls which have not survived.

Aegean influence appears again on the daggers, on the bowcase and on some of the gold-leaf chariot decorations, especially three small scenes of a beaked gryphon and a hunting dog leaping to attack an antelope (figure 56).

The sculptured reliefs in Horemheb's tomb at Saqqara are similar in style to the Luxor reliefs. They show a close affinity with tomb scenes at Amarna and with reliefs of Asiatic and Nubian enemies on Tutankhamun's gold chariot. Carefully observed portraits of individuals of different racial types capture details of age and expression. Similar care is displayed in painted scenes of Nubians in Huya's tomb at Thebes and in reliefs from Ay's chapel at Karnak (figure 57). A set of gaming sticks in the tomb has carvings of female prisoners, both African and Syrian, which resemble the bound female captives below Queen Tiye's throne in the Theban tomb of Kheruef (no.142). Interest in racial types remained part of Egyptian official art but the relaxed style was retained only in the defeated melée of a battle scene. Similarly, the relaxed poses of royal figures did not continue into the Nineteenth Dynasty.

Tutankhamun's canopic chest is protected by four goddesses

55. Wooden casket with painted scenes of Tutankhamun in his chariot attacking Syrian enemies (side) and desert animals (lid), from the Antechamber. See figure 5. (Cairo Museum, Carter 21. Photograph by Frances Welsh.)

56. A winged gryphon and a hunting dog attack an antelope in 'flying leap' pose, on gold appliqué from horse harness. (Carter 122.w. Drawing by R. B. Welsh.)

with Amarna-style figures, each of whom stands poised on the balls of her feet as she turns her head sideways, pressing her body close to the side she is protecting with her outstretched arms. The suggestion that these figures were planned to represent the queen in her protective role is reinforced by the orthodox representation of the goddesses in relief on the shrine (figures 46 and 50). The carved figures of winged goddesses which stand at each corner of Tutankhamun's sarcophagus fit a sequence of development linking the Amarna royal sarcophagus with those of Ay and Horemheb.

The return to traditional style in religious iconography seems to

57. Relief of Nubians captured by Tutankhamun, on a sandstone block from the dismantled chapel at Karnak. (Photograph by Frances Welsh.)

have been accomplished easily by the same craftsmen who found the changes in royal iconography confusing. On the stela in Horemheb's tomb at Saqqara the three traditional gods are slim figures in classic dress but Horemheb appears before them with the figure and dress

58. Pectoral ornament symbolising the birth of the Sun and the Moon with Tutankhamun between Thoth and Re-Harakhty in the solar disk at the apex of a triangular design of leaves and fruits with a chalcedony scarab at centre; gold and semi-precious stones. (Cairo Museum; Carter 267.d. Drawing by R. B. Welsh.)

59. Three-dimensional pectoral ornament representing sunrise, with the scarab and the sundisk in the solar barque, suspended on flexible straps of separate inlaid gold plaques held by rows of small beads; lapis lazuli, carnelian, felspar and turquoise in gold. (Cairo Museum; Carter 267.g.h. Photograph by Frances Welsh.)

of an Amarna official.

The formality of traditional Egyptian design and decorative motifs and the preference for balance were not deflected by the freedom introduced in Amarna art: heaped offerings in the Luxor reliefs are arranged in a defined pattern; elements of the Nebkheperure rebus are transposed, where necessary, to fit the design of jewellery; flowers and vegetation form neat clumps and stylised bouquets; even where animals are shown in freely leaping poses, they are confined within a border, as on the bowcase.

Jewellery designs are traditional and symbolic and echo those of the Middle Kingdom. Elements of Tutankhamun's prenomen are combined with royal emblems and arranged into balanced patterns or blocks on bracelets, pectorals and earrings (figure 58). The scarab (*khepri*), often winged, features prominently as a central motif or is used repeatedly to unify the design, as on the pectoral whose scarab motif is repeated on its suspension straps (figure 59). To fill a circular space, the wings of the scarab sweep upwards and inwards to unite the sundisk (Re) with the design (figure 60).

Large surface areas are given texture and variation by the use of bands of alternately repeated patterns of varying widths (figure 61) and the long palmette is adjusted to fit the space available (figure

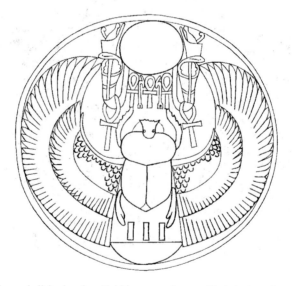

60. Gilded wood disk showing Nebkheperure in a unified design; from the head of the falcon model standing on the yoke bar of a chariot. (Cairo Museum; Carter 160. Drawing by R. B. Welsh.)

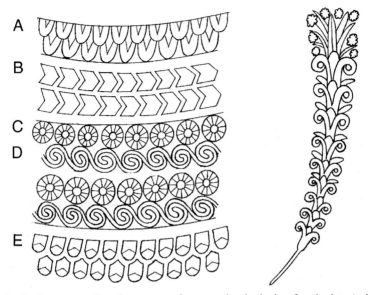

61 (Left). Patterns used on large areas, for example, the body of a chariot: A, leaf; B, chevron; C, rosette; D, running spiral; E, feather pattern or *rishi*. (Drawing by R. B. Welsh.)
62 (Right). Palmette design adaptable to fit available space. (Drawing by R. B. Welsh.)

62), as on the dagger sheath or the curved edge of a chariot. The running spiral, chevron and palmette designs, deriving from eastern Mediterranean models, are prominent on military equipment.

Architectural links

The architecture of religious buildings reflects religious beliefs and is governed by the rituals to be performed within them. Return to the orthodox religion of Amun included a return to the traditional style of temple architecture. The cult of the Aten required large unroofed areas with altars exposed to the sun's rays instead of the small inner sanctuary where the cult image of the god lay hidden from view. Although temples before and after the Amarna period included small unroofed sun chapels, the primary aim of the traditional temple was to evoke the mythical papyrus thicket on the primeval mound of creation, by protecting the god's essence behind a series of closed doors and lowering ceilings.

Tutankhamun's architects achieved a compromise by following Amenhotep III's earlier building style of open courtyards with colonnades of graceful columns in front of roofed halls and the sanctuary. Heavy open-papyrus columns appear to have been a late innovation of Amenhotep III, who built a double row as a portico for Luxor Temple. Tutankhamun's temple at Faras appears to have imitated Luxor Temple to symbolise continuity with Amenhotep III. Slim closed-bud papyrus-bundle columns were used. Straight, fluted columns with vertical bands of inscription were used at Kawa. Slim papyrus columns were placed in the tomb chapels of Horemheb and Maya at Saqqara. Resembling small temples with pylon gateways, colonnaded courtyards and inner sanctuary, this design continued. The heavy papyrus-bundle columns introduced under Amenhotep III (Theban tomb no. 55 Ramose) and used in Amarna tombs lapsed, but the heavy single-papyrus column, with open- or closed-bud capital, was adopted for Nineteenth Dynasty temples.

Tomb design conformed to the restored cults. At Thebes the private tomb continued to be a rock-cut chamber with a transverse vestibule above a deep burial shaft. Royal tombs included the sequence of chambers required for the Osiris cult and, in order to reflect the increasingly important cult of the sun god Re, they were henceforth arranged along a straight axis like the Royal Tomb at Amarna. Thus, Tutankhamun, the last member of the royal family devoted to the Aten, was denied a straight-axis tomb while his orthodox successors adopted this Amarna innovation for themselves.

7
Historical aftermath

The apparently unexpected death of Tutankhamun created a political problem which repeated the crisis at the time of his accession. The two mummified babies enclosed in separate nests of coffins and placed in the Treasury seem to indicate that Ankhsenamun was the sole survivor of the Eighteenth Dynasty royal line. Although she could have acted as regent for a young male relative as Queen Hatshepsut had done, sole rule was not feasible.

To prevent political and economic collapse, the high officials who controlled Egypt seem to have agreed to support a non-royal claimant, Ay, as Pharaoh. There is no evidence for internal strife at this time. This may confirm the suggestion that the King's Regent Horemheb was fighting the Hittites in Syria at the time, with limited success. Ay had no right to the throne but his accession could be legitimated by his performance of funerary rites for his predecessor (as Horus caring for his father Osiris) and also by marriage to the Royal Heiress.

It seems that Ankhsenamun did not wish to marry Ay. A document in the Hittite state archive describes a letter received from the widowed Great Royal Wife requesting that a Hittite royal prince be sent to Egypt to be her husband, which would mean she did not have to marry a subject. This letter appears to have been from Ankhsenamun, writing during the period of mourning after Tutankhamun's death. However, the incredulity of the Hittites at this request caused a long delay, and when the Hittite prince Zannanza finally set out he was intercepted near the Egyptian border and killed, presumably by Egyptians. Such a marriage would have resulted in the Hittite domination of Egypt and could not have been countenanced.

Meanwhile, Tutankhamun's funeral rites had been performed by Ay, his tomb sealed and his widow Ankhsenamun probably joined in formal marriage to Ay. She then disappears from the record and Ay's original wife, Nefertiti's nurse Tey, accompanies him in his tomb scenes.

The policies of Tutankhamun were continued and, although Ay replaced Tutankhamun's name on many reliefs and statues with his own, there was no attempt to obliterate records or destroy the tomb, which was tidied and re-sealed when it was found to have been robbed. Ay also built a memorial chapel at the temple at Karnak in honour of Tutankhamun.

When Ay died after about four years, Horemheb's control of the

63. Sandstone block from Ay's chapel at Karnak Temple, with Nebkheperure Tutankhamun in cartouches partially erased. (Photograph by Frances Welsh.)

army ensured his smooth accession. The return to orthodox religion and political stability had been accomplished and Horemheb took credit for this by inserting his name on Tutankhamun's Restoration Stela. He dated his reign from the end of that of Amenhotep III to exclude from the records all kings with Amarna connections and placed his name on their monuments and statues. He demolished temples built at Karnak by Akhenaten, Tutankhamun and Ay (figure 63) but Tutankhamun's tomb remained inviolate. He may have obliterated visible reminders of Akhenaten's regime to ensure his political safety as he had no direct heir.

He chose as his successor his vizier, who took the throne as Ramesses I and founded a new dynasty – the Nineteenth. His robust and able descendants led Egypt into a period of prosperity and empire. These kings, who had no loyalty to the cult of Aten, instigated a systematic destruction of everything associated with it, especially the site of Akhetaten, but time and chance had by then caused the location of Tutankhamun's tomb to be forgotten and hidden from intruders until the twentieth century AD.

64. North-west corner of the Burial Chamber: the wall painting shows Tutankhamun and his Ka being greeted by Osiris; below is the sarcophagus containing the outer coffin to which the mummy was returned after examination. The wall niches are for magical bricks and statuettes. (Photograph by Frances Welsh.)

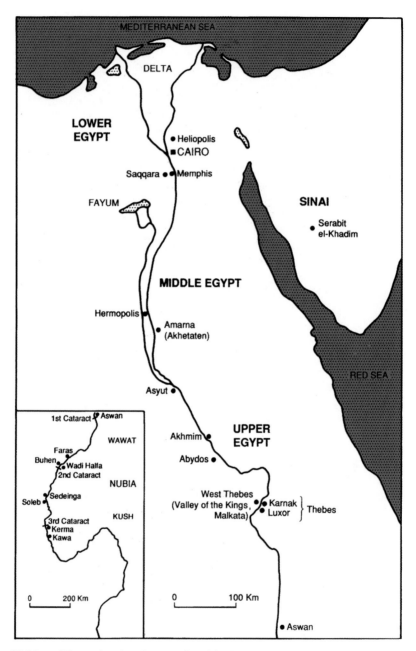

65. Map of Egypt showing sites mentioned in the text. (Map by Robert Dizon.)

8
Further reading

Carter, H. *The Tomb of Tutankhamen*, volumes 1 to 3 (volume 1 with A. C. Mace). Cassell, London, 1923, 1927, 1933.

This is the excavator's detailed account of the discovery and clearance of the tomb and his description of the contents as found. These volumes are the primary source for studying the tomb, together with the excavation records and other papers of Howard Carter concerning the tomb's discovery and clearance, which are at the Griffith Institute, Oxford, which sponsors publication of specialist studies in the Tut'ankhamun's Tomb series.

Books dealing with this subject in a general way are readily available. The following selection reflects modern research and studies of specific aspects, most having specialist bibliographies to assist the serious student.

Selected books

Aldred, C. *Jewels of the Pharaohs*. Thames & Hudson, 1971.
Aldred, C. *Akhenaten, King of Egypt*. Thames & Hudson, 1986.
Allen, S. J. *Tutankhamun's Tomb*. Metropolitan Museum of Art, New York, 2006. Photos by Harry Burton.
Andrews, C. *Ancient Egyptian Jewellery*. British Museum Publications, 1990.
Davies, N. M., and Gardiner, A. H. *Tomb of Huy, Viceroy of Nubia in the Reign of Tutankhamun, No. 40*. Egypt Exploration Society, 1926.
Desroches-Noblecourt, C. *Tutankhamen: Life and Death of a Pharaoh*. The Connoisseur and Michael Joseph, 1963.
Eaton-Krauss, M. *The Sarcophagus in the Tomb of Tut'ankhamun*. Oxford, 1993.
Eaton-Krauss, M., and Graefe, E. *The Small Golden Shrine from the Tomb of Tut'ankhamen*. Griffith Institute, Oxford, 1985.
Edwards, I. E. S. *Treasures of Tutankhamun*. Exhibition catalogue, Thames & Hudson, 1972.
El-Khouli, Ali, et al. *Stone Vessels, Pottery and Sealings from the Tomb of Tut'ankhamun*. Oxford University Press, 1993.
Fox, P. *Tutankhamun's Treasure*. Oxford University Press, 1951.
Hepper, F. N. *Pharaoh's Flowers; Plants of Tutankhamun's Tomb*. HMSO, 1990.

Hoving, T. *Tutankhamun: The Untold Story*. Simon & Schuster, New York, 1978.

Jones, D. *Model Boats from the Tomb of Tut'ankhamun*. Tut'ankhamun's Tomb series, IX; Griffith Institute, Oxford, 1990.

Lee, C. C. *The Grand Piano Came by Camel: Arthur C. Mace, the Neglected Egyptologist*. Mainstream Publishing, 1992. Includes Mace's substantial contribution to the conservation and recording of objects from the tomb.

Leek, F. F. *The Human Remains from the Tomb of Tut'ankhamun*. Tut'ankhamun's Tomb series, V: Griffith Institute, Oxford, 1972.

Lesko, L. H. *King Tut's Wine Cellar*. B C Scribe Publications, 1977.

Littauer, M. A., and Crouwel, J. H. *Chariots and Related Equipment from the Tomb of Tut'ankhamun*. Tut'ankhamun's Tomb series, VIII; Griffith Institute, Oxford, 1985.

Martin, G. T. *The Hidden Tombs of Memphis*. Thames & Hudson, 1991. Detailed description of the tombs of Horemheb and Maya at Saqqara.

Murray, H., and Nuttall, M. *A Handlist of Howard Carter's Catalogue of Objects in Tut'ankhamun's Tomb*. Tut'ankhamun's Tomb series, I; Griffith Institute, Oxford, 1963.

Piankoff, A. *The Shrines of Tutankh-amon* (editor, N. Rambova). Princeton University Press, 1955.

Reeves, C. N. (editor). *After Tutankhamun*. Kegan Paul International, 1991. Papers given at the conference held at Highclere Castle in 1990.

Reeves, C. N. *The Complete Tutankhamun*. Thames & Hudson, 2007. A detailed survey of objects in the tomb with comprehensive bibliography of articles in journals.

Tait, W. J. *Game Boxes and Accessories from the Tomb of Tut'ankhamun*. Tut'ankhamun's Tomb series, VII; Griffith Institute, Oxford, 1982.

Weigall, A. *Tutankhamun and Other Essays*. Butterworth, 1923.

Wiese, A., and Brodbeck, A. (editors). *Tutankhamun. The Golden Beyond* (exhibition catalogue). Antikenmuseum Basel und Sammlung, 2004.

Wilkinson, A. *Ancient Egyptian Jewellery*. Methuen, 1971.

Winlock, H. E. *Materials Used at the Embalming of King Tut-ankhamun*. Metropolitan Museum of Art, New York, 1941.

9

Museums

The material from Tutankhamun's tomb is in the care of the Egyptian Antiquities Service, a major part being displayed in the Egyptian Antiquities Museum in Cairo, with a selection of items in the Luxor Museum of Egyptian Art. The mummy lies inside the outermost coffin in the sarcophagus in his tomb in the Valley of the Kings. Statuary and objects relating to Tutankhamun's reign and the Amarna Period are held in museum collections elsewhere, including those given below. Intending visitors are advised to check opening times before making a special journey.

United Kingdom

The British Museum, Great Russell Street, London WC1B 3DG. Telephone: 020 7323 8000. Website: www.thebritishmuseum.ac.uk

Fitzwilliam Museum, Trumpington Street, Cambridge CB2 1RB. Telephone: 01223 332900. Website: www.fitzmuseum.cam.ac.uk

The Petrie Museum of Egyptian Archaeology, University College London, Malet Place, London WC1E 6BT. Telephone: 020 7679 2884. Website: www.petrie.ucl.ac.uk

National Museum of Scotland, Chambers Street, Edinburgh EH1 1JF. Telephone: 0131 247 4422. Website: www.nms.ac.uk

The Victoria and Albert Museum, Cromwell Road, South Kensington, London SW7 2RL. Telephone: 020 7942 2000. Website: www. vam.ac.uk Textiles.

Belgium

Musées Royaux d'Art et d'Histoire, Parc du Cinquantenaire, 10, 1000 Brussels. Website: www.kmkg-mrah.be/newfr/index.asp

Denmark

Ny Carlsberg Glyptotek, Dantes Plads 7, DK-1556 Copenhagen V. Website: www.glyptoteket.dk

Egypt

Egyptian Antiquities Museum, Tahrir Square, Cairo. Website: www. egyptianmuseum.gov.eg

Luxor Museum of Egyptian Art, Sharia Nahr el-Nil, Luxor.

Museum of Ancient Agriculture, el-Dokki, Giza, Cairo.

France
Musée du Louvre, Palais du Louvre, F-75041 Paris. Website: www. louvre.fr

Germany
Ägyptisches Museum und Papyrus-sammlung, Altes Museum, Am Lustgarten, 10178 Berlin-Mitte. Website: www.smb-spk-berlin. de
Staatliche Sammlung Ägyptischer Kunst, Meiserstrasse 10, 80333 Munich. Website: www.aegyptisches-museum-muenchen.de

Italy
Museo Civico Archiologico, Via dell'Archiginnasio 2, 40124, Bologna. Website: www.comune.bologna.it/museoarcheologico
Museo Egizio, Palazzo dell'Accademia delle Scienze, Via Accademia delle Scienze 6, 10123 Turin. Website: www.museoegizio.it

Netherlands
Rijksmuseum van Oudheden, Rapenburg 28, 2311 EW Leiden, Zuid Holland. Website: www.rmo.nl

Sudan
Sudan National Museum, Sharia'a el Nil, Khartoum.

United States of America
The Brooklyn Museum, 200 Eastern Parkway, Brooklyn, New York, NY 11238-6052. Website: www.brooklynmuseum.org
Metropolitan Museum of Art, 1000 Fifth Avenue at 82nd Street, New York, NY 10028. Website: www.metmuseum.org
Museum of Fine Arts, Avenue of the Arts, 465 Huntington Avenue, Boston, Massachusetts 02115-5597. Website: www.mfa.org
University of Chicago Oriental Institute Museum, 1155 East 58th Street, Chicago, Illinois 60637. Website: www.oi.uchicago.edu/museum
Penn Museum, University of Pennsylvania Museum of Archaeology and Anthropology, 3620 South Street, Philadelphia, Pennsylvania PA 19104. Website: www.museum.upenn.edu

Index

Page numbers in italics refer to illustrations